San Francisco
from the air

ANTONIO ATTINI   FABRIZIO GUGLIELMINI

vmb
PUBLISHERS

San Francisco
from the air

CONTENTS

1 The elegant clock tower alongside the Embarcadero dates back to 1898. It was restored to its former glory in 2003.

2-3 The office towers of downtown San Francisco stand out against the sky in the background; in the foreground, North Beach, Fisherman's Wharf and the Marina area.

4-5 and 6-7 The principal landmarks in these two views of the Financial District are the San Francisco-Oakland Bridge (the Bay Bridge), opened in 1936, and the 853-foot Transamerica Pyramid.

8 Downtown emerges above the fog that often envelops the city.

9 The Golden Gate, one of the world's most famous bridges, was built in 1937.

10-11 Breakers roll up against the coastline of Inner Richmond (top) and Outer Richmond (bottom).

12-13 A Golden Gate Bridge tower visible above the morning fog.

VMB Publishers®
An imprint of White Star, Italy

© 2005 White Star S.p.A.
Via Candido Sassone, 22/24 - 13100 Vercelli, Italy
www.whitestar.it
Revised edition in 2005

ISBN 10: 88 540 0578 9
ISBN 13 978 88 540 0578 5
Reprints:
2 3 4 5 6   09 08 07 06
TRANSLATION TEXTS: TIMOTHY STROUD
TRANSLATION CAPTIONS: SARAH PONTING
Printed in Indonesia
Color separation by Chiaroscuro, Turin

Photographs Antonio Attini

Text Fabrizio Guglielmini

Graphic Design Marinella Debernardi

Introduction

Spanning the entrance to one of the world's most spectacular bays, the Golden Gate is the symbol of multifaceted San Francisco. From under its ocher-red arches the Californian metropolis, a crossroads of cultures both historically and geographically, looks out across the Pacific Ocean toward the Far East. San Francisco also opens onto the natural beauties of its enormous bay, with which it has existed in symbiosis since its foundation in 1776. The city's short but rich history began with Spanish missionaries and soldiers, and in recent years, after many social and political shifts, has evolved to encompass the technological world of personal computers and the web economy. Its districts are spread over forty or so hills, including North Beach, Chinatown, and the old hippy area of Haight-Ashbury with its Victorian houses. These districts represent the chapters in a history that has as its leading characters the pioneers of the 1850s Gold Rush, Asian communities, Europeans, yuppies and the urban tribes of the new century, in a scenario featuring the Internet, new fashions, and contemporary political movements. Steep streets, some positively precipitous, climb and drop through the districts and are an integral part of the city's spectacular charm.

Unlike New York or Los Angeles, life in San Francisco has maintained two rhythms: that of a large international metropolis and that of a city that has not forgotten that it is built for people. Loyal to its history, San Francisco has never lost sight of its cosmopolitan vocation as a bridge to Asia and a vacation destination for millions of Europeans. And for decades neighboring Berkeley with its university has represented a political and cultural point of reference for generations of young people all over the world.

San Francisco is a city with many different faces. Its Oriental one can be discovered in Chinatown, the 24-block district that is home to the world's second-largest community of Chinese expatriates, following that of New York. This city- within-a-city is entered through the spectacular Dragon's Gate on Grant Avenue. San Francisco's European face can be found in the coffee bars lining Columbus Avenue; these were founded to alleviate the homesickness of the many

Italians who arrived in the city at the beginning of the last century to seek their fortunes. While explorations of the ethnic districts are invaluable to an understanding of the city, visitors should not forget that San Francisco also features residential areas, such as Pacific Heights and the peaceful streets of Cole Alley, far away from the surging crowds of vacationers.

To the east of the city lies the bay, which boasts an enviable ecological equilibrium; to the west lies the ocean, and, in-between, the fast-moving fog that closes in or lifts to provide unexpected views of the hills as far as Twin Peaks, or rows of Victorian houses that contrast with downtown's modern skyline dominated by the Transamerica Pyramid. The Bay Area contributes to this aesthetic and environmental experience (due to its natural blessings and plethora of landscapes), from wealthy Marin County to wild Point Reyes, and inland, with the vineyards of the Napa and Sonora Valleys, consecrated to the production of fine red and white wines able to compete with the best South African, Chilean and Australian labels.

Since the 1950s, San Francisco has been the breeding ground of many of the alternative cultures and politics of America and, sometimes, the world; it acts as a beacon for the ideals and dreams of millions of young people. It has spawned cultures, counter-cultures and movements such as the Beat Generation and the 1967 Summer of Love. Here, in this stronghold and think-tank of the Democrats and in nearby Berkeley, at the same time as declarations of Peace and Love were being made, student revolts erupted at the end of the 1960s, along with the establishment of the Afro-American Black Panther movement and the gay community. Tolerant – and consequently often affected by social and racial tensions – San Francisco is home to the intellectuals of the left, political activists, organizations of the homeless, and the leading lights of the personal computer industry. Today it is undergoing a period of transition: after the boom of Silicon Valley and the web economy of the '90s, today the city is reinventing itself with new urban projects such as the conversion of the Presidio military zone into a national park and the new baseball stadium, home of the San Francisco Giants, in SBC Park.

15 Columbus Avenue cuts the city into two. In the foreground are small, older buildings of North Beach, traditional home of the city's Italian community. Beyond is the downtown area, dominated by the Transamerica Pyramid.

16 San Francisco, looking north. The huge bay flanks the city on the east; at the top of the picture can be seen the slender thread of the Golden Gate Bridge.

17 top San Francisco Peninsula and Bay in their entirety. At the base of the photograph is Monterey Bay, made famous by John Steinbeck.

17 bottom North of the Golden Gate Bridge is the *bohemian-artistic town of Sausalito; jutting into the Pacific is the Pt. Reyes peninsula; directly east of San Francisco, reached by the Bay Bridge are Oakland and Berkeley.*

18-19 San Francisco has a special relationship with the hours of the day. When the city's lights are on and the Californian sky changes color, the panorama becomes enchantingly *beautiful. Brightly lit Market Street cuts diagonally across this view, while the Bay Bridge can be seen on the right.*

20-21 San Francisco's downtown business center, glowing in the light of the blazing sunset. Besides the unmistakable silhouette of the Transamerica Pyramid, another important landmark can be seen on the right: the 758-foot Bank of America Building.

Contemporary culture in San Francisco also has many facets, and is imbued with a vitality that has always helped it to stay alive, even during the hardest times. The face of the metropolis has not only been changed by the new stadium, but also by the building on Third Street that houses the Museum of Modern Art, designed by Swiss architect Mario Botta. Other significant projects include the recent rebuilding of the Contemporary Jewish Museum by Daniel Libeskind and the new premises of another historic exhibition venue, the M.H. de Young Memorial Museum, designed by the architectural firm Herzog & de Meuron.

The city's theaters also offer an alternative reading of the metropolis: from the Magic Theater, where for many years Sam Shepard was playwright-in-residence, to the Orpheum, where Broadway blockbusters are staged. Numerous famous writers are also associated with San Francisco: they range from Mark Twain, who came to the city to work as a journalist, to Jack London, who was born in Brannan Street. However, the man who made the greatest single contribution to San Francisco's literary legend was Dashiell Hammett, an ex-detective, who from the 1920s onward immortalized the city in his stories, the most famous of which is *The Maltese Falcon*. Appreciations of San Francisco are many, and Marguerite Yourcenar, the French writer and untiring traveler, penned powerful words on the city and its Victorian homes: "The houses of San Francisco, surmounted by disquieting skyscrapers here and there, have conserved their human dimension for the most part, and their pastel shades of blue, white, pink and pistachio green give the streets the appearance of ice cream in different flavors."

Although the city's Silicon Valley makes it one of the world's most advanced technological capitals, San Francisco keeps its history alive for the pleasure of residents and visitors alike, restoring its static wealth of historical houses celebrated by Yourcenar and its "mobile assets," such as the cable cars that continue to offer extraordinary views from Russian Hill and Nob Hill. And it has done so by emphasizing the city's innately scenic spirit created by the unique juxtaposition of its lush natural setting and the works of man.

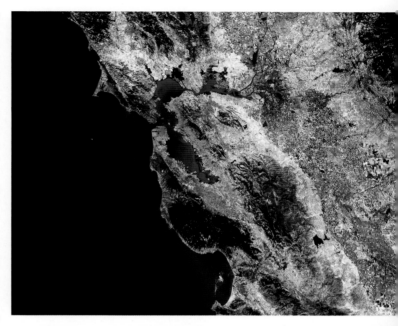

DOWNTOWN

When seen from the air, San Francisco's perfect adaptation of layout to the geography of the peninsula it lies on becomes dramatically clear: its skyscrapers, Victorian houses and suburbs roll on down the 40-mile strip of land bounded by the Pacific to the west and San Francisco Bay to the east.

The city's earliest section had its origins in the plan developed in 1847 by the civil engineer Jasper O'Farrell. Though O'Farrell was laying down streets on land that was as yet little used, his successors were able (either by choice or fortuitousness) to maintain a balance between nature and the districts that slowly grew to take in the new residents, until the city's present population of 800,000 was reached. The result is that the city still has the green areas of Golden Gate Park and its Panhandle (a strip of land like the handle to the pan-shaped park) to the west of the city, the area of the Presidio National Park to the northwest, the coast from Baker Beach to China Beach, and Lincoln Park.

Downtown lies between Market Street and Van Ness Avenue. Like in all large American cities, it has a high concentration of financial and business activities and skyscrapers. Banks and companies are based at its western end while political power is represented at the eastern end by the Civic Center, dominated by the huge gilded dome of the Civic Hall.

The Financial District begins at Justin Herman Plaza and stretches to the Transamerica Pyramid that overlooks North Beach. Awash with traffic until early evening – when it turns into a ghost town – the Financial District revolves around Montgomery Street and Pine Street, onto which the Pacific Coast Stock Exchange faces. Another landmark is the 758 feet of the Bank of America skyscraper (though the bank has not been its owner for many years) with its 200-ton monolithic sculpture *Transcendence* by the Japanese sculptor Masayuki Nagare. Next to the Transamerica and Bank of America buildings are other steel and concrete towers that have reshaped the Bay Area's skyline over the past 80 years.

A short distance from the unmistakable profile of the Transamerica Pyramid, brick-lined Jackson Square is the historical symbol of San Francisco's pioneering era, the Gold Rush and the city's first millionai-res. Compared to the long span of European history, 150 years is not a very long time but here such a span harks back to San Francisco's origins and its "mythical" founding. Buildings that date to 1850 – many of which survived the 1906 earthquake – stand on four blocks between Washington Street, Columbus Avenue and Sansome Street. No. 472 Jackson was the first French Consulate (1852), and the buildings that were home to the Hotaling distillery also survived the fire of 1906. A few steps on at No. 415 stands the first building (1893) occupied by the chocolate-producer Domingo Ghirardelli, who built his empire in San Francisco.

The city's political center, symbolized by the golden dome of City Hall, is surrounded by cultural institutions. Constructed in 1915 by James Rolph Jr., the highly active mayor of the time, it is flanked by the large Opera House and the old Public Library. All the buildings are of monumental dimensions, and particularly large if compared to the geographical size and population of the city.

The Square's history began in 1850 at the time of San Francisco's first city plan, and it received its name during the Civil War. Over the decades, Union Square became one of the most important meeting points in the city. It gave comfort to those travelers who, thinking they were in a European-style city, looked for the "center."

Macy's, the most traditional of the large American stores, and the famous Westin St. Francis Hotel (which lines the entire west side) face onto the square. The St. Francis was founded in 1904 and survived both the earthquake and fire of 1906. Its name is linked to the visits of many American presidents (including Nixon and Reagan) and other important politicians.

Union Square is an important tourist attraction to also draws residents out for a stroll in the city center. Like any public place of interest, Union Square is constantly at the center of debate: most of its garden areas have been done away with to discourage the homeless (which has drawn criticism), but everyone agrees that its night-time illumination, added to by the constant passing of the Powell–Mason cable car, is attractive.

The theater zone, with the historic names of the Geary Theater (1909) and the Curran Theater (1922)

lies just a few steps away from the square between Powell, Mason and Taylor streets.

Between Larkin and Market, close to Union Square, is an area best not entered at night: this is the Tenderloin, a squalid zone of crime and prostitution very different to the historic sociability of Union Square. But even the Tenderloin has its own fascination: its decadent bars, clubs and hotels make it a perfect setting for a film noir, and the walls of a number of buildings have murals of coastal, street and exotic scenes.

Well off the tourist circuit, following the southward diagonal line formed by Market Street, Mission and Castro are colorful residential districts. Mission Dolores lies at the center of historic San Francisco; its Catholic mission dates back to 1776. Today Mission is served by South Van Ness, Mission and Valencia Streets. Since the early 1990s it is no longer just home to immigrants from Central and South America but has also been discovered by upper-middle-class whites as a result of the strong demand for housing in the city during the boom years of the web economy. Certain features date from the 1970s and '80s, such as the hip coffee bars where one can read, write and listen to music, or the alternative bookstores, which reflect the old fondness of young progressives for this zone of the city. However, once again it is the visual aspect that triumphs: Mission is literally covered with murals painted on houses that date back to the 1920s and '30s. Some of the most famous include those dedicated to Carlos Santana (on 22nd Street and Van Ness Avenue), the local Carnival (24th Street and Van Ness Avenue) and the political "500 years of resistance" in which Mexican Father Miguel Hidalgo is portrayed with Martin Luther King (24th and Florida Streets). Many of the more than 200 murals in the district date from the 1970s and were inspired by those painted by Diego Rivera for the San Francisco Art Institute.

Other distinctive features of the district are Mission Dolores Park, which housed two Jewish museums up until 1905, and the street life on 24th Street, made vibrant by the city's various ethnic groups, which range from Mexicans to Chileans. Their native traditions are reflected in restaurants, loud music and "homespun" centers that represent the Latino microcosm in Mission. Castro, the capital of the city's gay and lesbian communities (roughly 120,000 of its 800,000 residents), commences a few blocks away toward Market, between 17th and Noe Streets,. It is a city within a city, with its own customs and colors, and offers everything needed by a community that has exerted a great cultural influence since the '50s, and a political sway that no mayor can ignore since the '70s.

The office and workshop of the NAMES Project is at 2362 Market Street: this is an enormous panel almost a mile long that symbolizes all the victims of AIDS, the virus that threatened to annihilate the gay community and the life of the entire district during the late 1980s. The Project is composed of over 50,000 fabric panels featuring objects, photographs and memories of AIDS victims. Anyone wishing to contribute a panel to the project – which combines spontaneous art, social commitment and a funerary tribute – can do so at the NAMES office.

One of the district's key symbols is the Castro Theatre (on 17th and Castro Streets). This 1500-seat cinema was built in 1922 and designed by Timothy Pflueger in an extravagant fusion style that combines Hispanic elements with European eclecticism and Art Deco. The result is a style that seems expressly created for the aesthetic excesses of the district. The architectural mix of the interior is emphasized by stuccoes and oriental-style decorations and by the fluorescent colors of a Wurlitzer organ (made by the US company famous for its jukeboxes), whose music once accompanied silent films.

The center of the district, between 18th and 20th Streets, features many Victorian houses and eccentricities in the form of bookstores, restaurants and shops, as well as the growing "lesbo" presence of the Rainbow Flag community. The top of Twin Peaks, to the east of Castro, offers one of the finest of the city's numerous panoramic points (looking north and east), though the very best view has to be from the top of the Transamerica Pyramid.

Between Douglass and Dolores Streets there is an enclave within an enclave: far from the bustle of downtown, Noe Valley is an urban oasis for wealthy young whites, with peaceful restaurants and coffee bars frequented mainly by local residents.

26 A close-up of San Francisco's skyscrapers: this forest of buildings developed in the heart of downtown between Third Street and Embarcadero from the 1960s on.

28 left The huge Pacific Telesis Building rises on Third Street-Mission Street corner.

28 right This aerial view gives a clear idea of the proportions of the downtown skyscrapers. The Pacific Telesis building, for example – visible in the lower left corner – is put into perspective by the Standard Oil Building that towers over it.

29 Market Street, on the right in this view, cuts through a large part of downtown San Francisco. The dark shape of the Bank of America Building can be seen in front of the Transamerica Pyramid. In the foreground are the buildings constructed between the 1930s and the 1950s, which formed the original downtown area.

30 top and 30-31 Flying over downtown or visiting it on foot, the eye is inevitably drawn to the focal point of the city center: the Transamerica Pyramid.

31 top Beyond the pinnacle of the Pyramid, the island prison of Alcatraz emerges from the waters of the bay.

31 bottom The 777-foot Bank of America Building, completed in 1969, partially covers the Transamerica Pyramid, which marks the start of Columbus Avenue,

32-33 The Bay Bridge stretches out east of downtown. Part of the district at the foot of Telegraph Hill can be seen on the lower left.

34-35 A view of downtown: the lower buildings were constructed during the 1950s and '60s and the skyscrapers over the subsequent decades.

36 left Market Street cuts through downtown San Francisco as far as the Embarcadero.

36 right The skyscrapers of the Financial District seem to jostle for space, casting huge shadows. The urban development plan lays down strict regulations for the relative height and siting of high-rise buildings.

37 The massive Standard Oil Building (center) is surrounded by other skyscrapers in the area of downtown overlooking Mission Street.

38 The dark monolith of the Bank of America Building, left, stands next to the white tower of the Mandarin Oriental Hotel, surmounted by an aerial. This is one of the city's most luxurious hotels and is frequented by businessmen from all over the world.

38-39 A corner of downtown: this is the city's Financial District, the home of banks and multinationals, that overlooks the Embarcadero. It boasts 62 buildings over 330 feet tall.

39 top and 40-41 The spans of the Bay Bridge, reaching eastward cross San Francisco Bay toward Treasure Island and Oakland, are gradually revealed in these three photographs taken from the west and southwest at increasing heights. The Pacific Ocean is behind the viewer.

42 Downtown's architecture is a blend of old and new, creating a kind of stratification in which the lower buildings – which are generally the older ones – seem to have been swallowed up by the surrounding skyscrapers.

42-43 The terraces crowning the 43 stories of 333 Bush Street offer an unusual view of the downtown sky. The skyscraper was completed in 1986 and reflects the deconstructionist architecture of the decade.

44 Many different architectural styles coexist in downtown San Francisco. Some of the world's leading architects have worked in the city over the past decades, due to the presence of major clients such as banks and multinationals.

45 left In this eastward view, the Financial District's buildings peter out in the immediate area of the piers.

45 right The Embarcadero district can be seen beyond the last buildings of downtown, next to the bay.

46 top The Ferry
Building clock tower,
shown in the
foreground, precedes
the skyscrapers lining
the Embarcadero. The
reddish silhouette of
the Golden Gate
Bridge is visible in the
background.

46 bottom The low
Ferry Building, in
the center of the
photograph, for
many decades
ensured the
efficient movement
of goods and
passengers in the
bay.

46-47 The oval
Bayside Plaza is
dominated by the
Rincon Center, left.
The hills of the
Golden Gate
Recreation Area
can be seen in the
background,
beyond downtown.

48 top Urban redevelopment near the Ferry Building: the Embarcadero district, the romantic emblem of old San Francisco, is being gradually adapted to meet new requirements.

48-49 and 49 right The 236-foot clock tower of the Ferry Building was inspired by the architecture of a Moorish tower. It is not only an attractive building, but also a very strong one; it has remained standing through two destructive earthquakes.

49 top The Ferry Building was built in 1898. This pier was one of the bay's most important transport hubs and was used by 50 million passengers each year during the 1920s.

50-51 The Bay Bridge, shown here from the Financial District, is divided in two sections at Treasure and Yerba Buena islands. The city of Oakland can be seen in the background, stretching over the eastern shore of the bay.

52 Part of the
Yerba Buena
district seen from
the west: the red
building of the San
Francisco Museum
of Fine Art is
visible at the top.

53 top A shiny
metal dome marks
the corner of the

Keary Street
Building (center of
the photograph).
The 308-foot
structure was
completed in 1986
and is an excellent
yardstick for
getting an idea of
the relative heights
of the city's
buildings.

53 bottom
The futuristic
architecture of the
San Francisco
Museum of Modern
Art bounds one side
of the Yerba Buena
Gardens, which
host open-air
classical and jazz
concerts during the
summer.

54 top and 54-55 Union Square, one of the city's most popular squares for tourists and residents alike, features a series of shopping malls, theaters, hotels and restaurants.

54 center San Francisco's Chinatown – the largest in the world – covers the area between the

Financial District, to the east, and North Beach, to the north.

54 bottom The Rincon Center, a modern shopping mall with attractive and complex architecture, is a gourmet's paradise, with its Chinese, Korean, Indian, Italian and Thai restaurants.

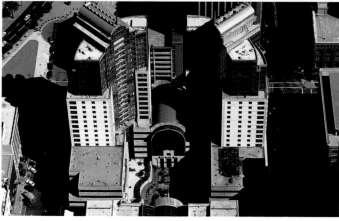

56 top St. Mary's Cathedral has an unusual roof that culminates in a huge cross reaching skyward, 190 feet above ground.

56 bottom The Episcopal Grace Cathedral is situated in San Francisco's elegant and historic Nob Hill district. A chapel had already been built on the same site in 1849, during the Gold Rush.

56-57 Flood Mansion, one of the luxurious testimonials to the ambition and power once wielded by San Francisco's ruling class, is now home to the Pacific Union Club.

57 top Overlapping circular roofs mark one of the temples built in Japantown, the city's Japanese enclave, which is principally dedicated to leisure and cultural activities.

58 The Civic Center features (top) the contrasting architectural styles of the War Memorial Veterans Building, housing the Herbst Theater, and the Louise M. Davies Symphony Hall (bottom), which offers a rich orchestral season.

58-59 and 59 top The dome of City Hall is the fifth largest in the world. It was completed in 1915 and has been considered the symbol of San Francisco's recovery from the 1906 earthquakes and fires ever since.

60-61 *The grandeur of the bay is plain to see in this photograph, showing the Civic Center at the bottom and Market Street on the right, above the entire Financial District.*

THE BAY AREA

The zone from Downtown to Fisherman's Wharf and Marina, the districts that line the bay to the north, reflects the complexity and variety of the cultures and ethnic groups that have mixed here over the past couple of centuries.

North Beach (the beach itself was removed in 1870 as part of the new urban planning scheme) centers on Columbus Avenue and is now dominated by the Transamerica Pyramid to the south. It is one of the city's historic districts, whose memories are chiefly preserved on Columbus Avenue, lined with many coffee bars featuring signs attesting to massive Italian immigration during the late 19th and early 20th centuries. History and tradition resonate in the premises of the Tosca Café, founded in far-off 1919, while the Vesuvio and the Trieste opened between 1949 and 1956, when the North Beach's first significant metamorphosis was under way, when it became the headquarters of the Beat generation, the standard bearers of a cultural and political movement. It is also the site of the legendary City Lights Bookstore, founded by the poet Lawrence Ferlinghetti in the 1950s with the ingenious and astoundingly innovative idea of selling paperbacks. Hundreds of intellectuals, along with world-famous figures like Jack Kerouac and Allen Ginsberg, would meet at North Beach to discuss revolutionary artistic manifestos and plan new cultural ventures under the guidance of their charismatic leaders. To cater to the growing influx of visitors from around the world, over the decades restaurants, jazz clubs and bars have opened alongside the city's coffee shops, above all on Grant Avenue, confirming the area's reputation for nightlife. Another meeting point is Washington Square: this is the site of the Sts. Peter and Paul Church and where at dawn –especially on weekends – Chinese residents practice the slow and ancient movements of tai chi chuan.

North Beach then climbs toward Telegraph Hill, which is lined with hundreds of pastel-colored hou-

ses and offers fine views over the entire bay. Atop the hill is Coit Tower, built with funds bequeathed by the eccentric millionaire Lillie Hitchcock Coit in 1933 to commemorate the city's firemen. She wished to pay them a tribute after having been a keen supporter all her life (she died in 1924 at the age of 87), even becoming an honorary member of the brigade. The tower houses 19 murals, painted in 1934, which represent various aspects of contemporary daily life in California. Nearby lies Chinatown with the enormous Chinatown Gate (also known as the Dragon's Gate) that looks onto Bush Street. The district seems to be built of layers of stores, shops, restaurants and houses between Powell and Kearney streets, and is dominated by the Tin How temple built in 1911. This is one of the symbols of the Chinese enclave (San Francisco's Chinese community is second only to that of New York) and overlooks Waverly Place, where exotic decoration reaches its height of glory in terms of colors and architecture.

The district's frenzied round-the-clock rhythm matches its inhabitants' inborn inclination for business, while Portsmouth Square is the hub of its social activity. The Far East Café is both a culinary and a historic point of reference. The restaurant was founded in the 1920s and is furnished with a profusion of dragons and red lanterns. While today's Chinatown is a miniature China with a tranquil routine, life has not always been so easy for its inhabitants. Having completed the construction of the transcontinental railroad in 1870, the first 12,000 inhabitants of Chinatown suffered discrimination that culminated in mob attacks in 1877. The politicians of the period played their part by voting through a law that prevented the reunification of Chinese families – an abuse that remained in force until 1943.

A short distance from the north section of Columbus Avenue, the visitor enters Russian Hill. This district of elegant houses overlooks North

Beach and the wharves of the Embarcadero, and is home to the San Francisco Art Institute. This building, the haunt of numerous art students, has a large hall adorned by Diego Rivera's *Making of a Mural*, which attracts visitors from all over the world. The peaceful Russian Hill district includes Lombard Street, famous for the eight steep hairpin curves in its spectacular descent from Hyde to Leavenworth. A long stairway runs parallel to this precipitous obstacle course, enabling pedestrians to descend from Hyde Street (a noted city's viewpoints) as far as Leavenworth.

Nob Hill and Pacific Heights lie inland from Russian Hill; on the bay side Fisherman's Wharf is the departure point for visits to the former Alcatraz Penitentiary, famous its sea-girt isolation and for such prisoners as Al Capone.

The origins of Nob Hill date back to 1873 when the arrival of the cable car made it the residential choice of the era's millionaires. Many of the Victorian houses built during the last few decades of the 19th century were destroyed by the 1906 fires: an exception was the Flood Mansion on California Street. Many buildings were later constructed in Edwardian style and the impressive Grace Cathedral between 1928 and 1964. Another residential district, Pacific Heights, beats all the others for its panoramic views and the luxuriousness of its houses. The Hass-Lilienthal House (1886) is a perfect example of Italianate Victorian architecture. The views between Van Ness and Presidio are spectacular and, toward the west, Presidio Heights is the continuation of the district and the most expensive area in terms of house prices.

A few blocks from Pacific Heights lies the city's other Oriental section: Japantown. Dominated by the Peace Pagoda, the district has many Buddhist temples and the famous Japanese-style Kabuki Hot Springs. A more recent addition is the Sokoji-Soto Zen Buddhist Temple, which was inaugurated in 1984 and reflects Zen practices and aesthetic principles.

Entertainment and leisure revolve around the Japan Center (built in 1968) and the Nihonmachi Mall, designed in the style of an ancient Japanese village and decorated with sculptures by the artist Ruth Asawa. Since the 1960s Japantown has been a cultural point of reference for the Japanese-American community. Unlike Chinatown, San Francisco's Japanese district is not a residential area, but a cultural magnet, where the local Japanese citizens come to enjoy their cuisine and practice their traditions. In April each year Japantown hosts the Cherry Blossom Festival, the community's major event. On the bay front, Fisherman's Wharf is a complex of piers, restaurants, shops and attractions that stretches from Pier 39 to Aquatic Park. For roughly 100 years from 1853, commercial shipping used this area, a little over a mile long. Pier 39 was built using weathered wood from abandoned piers (following the construction of the Golden Gate Bridge and the Bay Bridge) and was inspired by an old American coastal fishing village.

Today city residents call the Wharf a "tourist trap," but it attracts 12 million people a year. The Cannery between Fish Alley and Jefferson Street, another popular tourist attraction, was one of the first examples of an industrial building converted to commercial use featuring stores and restaurants. However, the great number of visitors is also due to the fact that these piers, located alongside dozens of other long-abandoned ones, are the departure point for visits to Alcatraz, the maximum-security island prison that was a federal penitentiary from 1934 to 1963. Today it is a museum where visitors can enter the prisoners' cells and yards. In 1979 the site was used to make the Clint Eastwood movie *Escape from Alcatraz*.

66 Tourists flock to winding Lombard Street, which cuts through the Russian Hill district, with a spectacular descent from Hyde to Leavenworth Street.

68 top Between 1853 and the 1950s, the piers of Fisherman's Wharf were used as docks.

68 bottom Pier 39 is the focal point of Fisherman's Wharf, a complex of piers, restaurants, shops and marine

attractions that draw 12 million people each year.

68-69 Pleasure craft throng Marina Yacht Harbor, seen here from the bay to the north, with the piers of Fisherman's Wharf on the far left.

69 top West of touristy Pier 39 are the abandoned wharves that were once used by San Francisco's ferry system, which was supplanted in the late 1930s by the bridges built over the bay.

70-71 The top of Telegraph Hill, the site of Coit Tower (foreground, right), offers splendid views over the spires of Sts. Peter and Paul Church, lower left and, center, busy Stockton and Powell streets.

72-73 Coit Tower was built with funds bequeathed by the millionaire Lillie Hitchcock Coit, as a tribute to the city's heroic firemen.

73 Part of the districts of Nob Hill and Pacific Heights can be seen in this view of North Beach and Coit Tower. The bay, with the orange silhouette of the Golden Gate Bridge, is visible in the background.

74-75 Victorian houses are found in many of the city's districts, but the Haight-Ashbury area has a particularly large number of them. The incentives offered by the city authorities have resulted in the restoration of many of these historical properties.

76-77 The long diagonal line of Columbus Avenue crosses the North

Beach district, traditional home of the Italian community, in the direction of the bay. Lower right, Washington Square in front of Sts. Peter and Paul Church.

78-79 The entire city, from downtown, left, to the residential districts of North Beach, Russian Hill, and Pacific Heights, in a single picture, taken from the bay.

80 top Greenery and residential blocks are two of the distinctive features of North Beach, which is still one of the city's most sought-after middle-class areas.

80 bottom Turntables are used to reverse the direction of the cable cars at the end of the lines. The first line was inaugurated in 1873 and the current 12 miles of track were renovated in 1984.

81 Nob Hill, adjoining North Beach, is one of the city's historic districts. The Mark Hopkins Hotel dominates the foreground; the Fairmont Hotel is behind it.

82-83 and 84-85 The façades of the houses in the heart of the North Beach district feature Victorian elements on more modern structures, with sunny bay windows.

*86 top and 86-87
One of the piers of
Fisherman's
Wharf: several
historic vessels are
moored at Hyde
Street Pier,
including the
Eureka ferryboat
and the Balclutha,
an imposing
three-masted
sailing ship.*

*86 bottom
The National
Maritime
Museum, with its
many naval
mementoes dating
back as far as the
mid-19th century,
is housed in a
building that
resembles a ship,
opposite Aquatic
Park.*

*87 top A detail of
Levi's Plaza, a
residential district
built in the 1980s
at the foot of
Telegraph Hill.*

*88-89 Pier 39, in
the heart of
Fisherman's Wharf,
is one of the city's*

*main tourist
attractions. The
complex, built on
an old loading
quay constructed
in 1905, is a
reconstruction of a
fishing village,
made from the
weathered wood of
abandoned piers.*

*90 and 91
Fisherman's Wharf
is the departure
point for visits to
Alcatraz Island,
from 1934 to 1963
site of a federal
penitentiary. Today
the complex is a
museum and was
the set for the 1979
movie Escape from
Alcatraz. The
Cellhouse
(distinguished by its
flat blue roof) is
flanked by the
lighthouse, and the
exercise yard is
visible beyond.*

*92-93 Beyond
the piers of
Fisherman's
Wharf, Columbus
Avenue runs
diagonally from
the Cannery, a
former Del Monte
factory and now a
shopping mall, to
the foot of the
Transamerica
Pyramid. Left, the
Bay Bridge extends
out toward
Oakland.*

THE

GOLDEN GATE

Part open-air museum, part residential district. Psychedelic memories for tourists and rows of Victorian houses now inhabited by the well-to-do. An important part of San Francisco's recent history, Haight-Ashbury is the district that was home to the hippies during the famous Summer of Love in 1967 and became known the world over as the mecca of alternative cultures. Messages of peace, gatherings and the glorious concerts of the Grateful Dead are still celebrated in stores that sell records, books, clothes and photographs of the flower-children period. This is particularly the case in Haight Street, which the 'degenerate' heirs of the beatniks (according to the beatniks themselves) chose as their headquarters forty years ago. In recent decades, however, the clubs and restaurants have followed other trends, conforming with the fashions that come and go in San Francisco. Haight has acquiesced with this metamorphosis, with only its memories dedicated to the hippy era, the rest having become middle class. The multicolored spiral decorations have disappeared from the house-fronts, and the area has followed the same development upgrade experienced by SoMa and Mission. Between Buena Vista Park and the Panhandle, the Victorian houses have been returned to their old splendor, particularly as the local administration has offered new owners incentives to protect the city's architectural patrimony.

Like in many other parts of the city, the Great Depression brought decline to Haight, which, during the late 19th century and first decades of the 20th, had been a residential district. The low rents during the '50s attracted Afro-Americans and the avant-garde of the Beat generation. The next two decades were linked indissolubly to the hippy myth which from here fanned out around the world. And, despite later transformations, many of the addresses here still keep the myth alive: some of these are the Richard Spreckels Mansion (at 737 Buena Vista Avenue West), where Jack London lived at the start of the 20th century, roughly 70 years before musician Graham Nash set up a recording studio here. On Ashbury another Victorian building housed the musicians and followers of the Grateful Dead for all of 1966, while psychedelic paintings,

T-shirts and other hippy memorabilia can be seen in the Red Victorian Bed, Breakfast and Art (1665 Haight Street). A direct heir of the hippy years is the Haight-Ashbury Free Clinic, where free medical treatment is still provided today. In Lower Haight, a few blocks from the district, the large Alamo Square is another of the city's symbolic locations. Here the hills and views are very striking. The square is lined by the famous row of Victorian houses (between Hayes and Steiner Streets) where Nobel Prize-winner Toni Morrison lives, and which have the skyline of downtown as a backdrop.

Heading west towards the ocean from Haight, one comes to the green strip of the Panhandle just before Golden Gate Park. Since 1871 this gradually began to take the place of the low natural vegetation and the gigantic dunes that herald the Pacific. The Park's first warden, William Hammond Hall, had his work cut out to fight the coast's enemy No. 1, the wind, by planting thousands of plants chosen ad hoc. The strong gusts prevented any plants from growing, and this made the sandy soil unstable. The turning point came with the arrival of a famous and resolute individual, the Scot John McLaren, one of the 19th-century immigrants who contributed to the development of the city. McLaren was a botanist who had studied in Scotland. From 1887 to his death 56 years later, he designed and created the Golden Gate Park that we know today.

The city's largest and most famous park includes lakes, sports facilities, various botanical gardens and dozens of bike and horse-riding paths. Visited every Sunday by thousands of people, the park contains the large M. H. de Young Memorial Museum, San Francisco's oldest public museum, and the Asian Art Museum next door, with its immensely valuable collections. The M. H. de Young exhibits paintings and sculptures from the American continent and Oceania, and items of African art.

Another corner of great beauty, and one that illustrates the city's aptitude for peaceful coexistence, is the Japanese Tea Garden, symbolized by a five-story pagoda exhibited at the Panama-Pacific Exposition in 1915 and then moved here. A pole with nine rings at the top of the pagoda represents the nine Buddhist heavens that correspond to various divini-

94 and 95 from left to right The Golden Gate Bridge seen from Marin County, with San Francisco in the background. A view of the city from Ocean Beach, *on the western side of San Francisco. Temple Emanu-El, in the Presidio district. The Palace of Legion of Honor, which houses a fine arts museum.* *97 Highway 101 heads north over the Golden Gate Bridge, inaugurated in 1937, to Marin County side.*

ties. The sacred building stands in a Zen garden and close to a Tea House surrounded by plants looked after by the Japanese master Nagao Sakurai.

Golden Gate Park stretches seven miles from Upper Haight as far as the ocean and separates the districts of Richmond (to the north of the park) and Sunset (to the south). Seen from above, these two districts do not seem to offer much interest, looking like expanses of single- or two-story buildings lining 48 avenues; however, when seen from the ground, the situation changes. The many Chinese residents and restaurants in Inner Richmond make the district a new Chinatown, though it retains many traces of its previous communities of German and Irish immigrants. Further west, Outer Richmond is home to other ethnic groups: American Russians, Cambodians and Vietnamese. The westernmost point of the district, which borders on Lincoln Park, is the location of the Palace of the Legion of Honor, a museum that replicates the architecture of the building of the same name in Paris.

To the south of Golden Gate Park, Sunset is mostly a residential district built between the 1930s and post-war period as a further expansion of the city's historical center. To the south the two hills known as Twin Peaks (the first explorers called them El Pecho de la Chola, literally 'The breasts of the Indian girl') offer fine views over the northern and eastern sections of the city.

On the other side of Park Presidio Boulevard, the Richmond-Sunset area is joined to the former military Presidio (under federal administration), one of the areas being renovated by the city as part of its next step forward. The Presidio's magnificent position overlooking the Golden Gate itself, and its enormous expanse of land make it a very attractive prospect. Changes to the area include the arrival of new residents, the conversion of dozens of old military buildings to civil use, and the establishment of a hi-tech service industry. One of the first to choose to participate was the director George Lucas, who is investing in a center for production and cinematic technologies in the Letterman Hospital. In the meantime, advertising agencies and TV and film production companies are using the huge areas left vacant by the departed army as temporary movie sets.

98-99 *The north tower of the Golden Gate Bridge appears in all its splendor, while the central portion of the bridge is swathed in fog, except for the tip of the south tower. San Francisco stretches out in the background.*

100 and 101 top For hundreds of years the same fog that often completely or partially hides the Golden Gate Bridge concealed the entrance to the bay from the explorers who started to sail up the Pacific coast as early as the 16th century.

100-101 The Golden Gate Bridge "emerges" from the fog to join the area around Fort Baker, built in the 1850s to defend the city from possible attacks from the north that never materialized.

102-103 The bridge was designed to resist two overwhelming forces: ocean currents and strong winds.

104-105 The orange-red color of the bridge, which is repainted continuously, was chosen following a debate involving all of San Francisco's citizens.

106-107 The Golden Gate Bridge reaches out toward the green areas of the Presidio and the Golden Gate Park. The Bay Bridge can be seen the background.

108 top Golf courses stretch out behind Ocean Beach, which overlooks the Pacific between Baker Beach and the Presidio.

108 bottom The long rectangular Golden Gate Park fits into the regular street plans of the districts of Inner Richmond (above) and Outer Richmond.

109 The ocean waves lap Cliff House, a historic building near Sutro Heights Park.

110-111 Richmond started to develop along the sides of the Golden Gate Park during the 1900-1950s period to satisfy the growing demand for housing.

*112 top The
Dutch Windmill
is situated in the
part of the
Golden Gate
Park that skirts
the Esplanade,
the road running
parallel to Ocean
Beach.*

*112-113 The beauty
of the Golden Gate
Park is enhanced by
artificial lakes.
Fulton Street, which
skirts the northern
side of the park and
climbs up toward
downtown, can be
seen on the left.*

*113 right This
close-knit complex
of buildings in the
Golden Gate Park
is home to the
famous California
Academy of
Sciences, the first
scientific institution
in the West,
founded in 1853.*

*114-115 The
Conservatory of
Flowers is reminiscent
of the English glass
and cast-iron
greenhouses of the
early 20th century,
and the botanists of
the Golden Gate Park
have created stunning
landscaping.*

116 top Lincoln
Park, in the
northwestern
corner of San
Francisco, is one of
the city's favorite
green leisure areas.

The paths through
the park are ideal for
walking or cycling
and the area is also
home to museums
and places of
historical interest.

116 bottom and
116-117 A
spectacular
entrance
announces the
Neoclassic-style
Palace of Legion of
Honor, in Lincoln

Park. The building
was inaugurated in
1924 and houses
19th- and 20th-
century works of
art, including the
casts of Auguste
Rodin's Thinker.

*118 top This
northward view
includes part of
the Presidio
National Park. A
red dome,
marking Temple
Emanu-El, is
visible in the
lower block.*

*118 bottom North
of the Presidio
National Park, the
bay glistens with
the circular
building of the
Palace of Fine Arts,
upper right. Mount
Tamalpais rises up
in the background.*

*118-119 The
elegant circular
pavilion of the
Palace of Fine Arts
was one of the great
attractions of the
1915 International
Exposition. The
complex also houses
the Exploratorium,
which offers visitors
lessons in applied
science and
astronomy.*

*119 top Temple
Emanu-El, built in
1925, was inspired
by the church of
Hagia Sofia, in*

*Istanbul, and
topped with an
imposing dome.*

*120-121 The
exclusive Marina
district stretches
east of the Palace of
Fine Arts, in the
foreground. Above,
downtown San
Francisco appears
in its full glory,
stretching from the
center rightward.
The Bay Bridge can
be seen beyond,
with the city of
Oakland in the
background.*

OUTSKIRTS

To the north of San Francisco lies Marin County, to the northwest the vineyards of the Napa and Sonoma valleys, and over the Bay Bridge to the east is the Berkeley campus and Oakland's musical scene. To the north and east of the bay are the mudflat nature reserves, an ecosystem composed of salt marshes and areas of untamed fauna and flora, in perfect equilibrium between the waters of the bay and the mainland. These reserves are a birdwatcher's paradise, and offer surreal and lunar landscapes when viewed from above.

Farther south, toward Los Angeles, lies some of California's most famous scenery: the Big Sur ("the Big South") region, formed by rocky promontories and cliffs. This natural haven stretches for 90 miles along the Pacific coast.

Looking out from the center of San Francisco, the thoughtful visitor realizes that the city and its bay are surrounded by a natural environment of great beauty, largely protected from urban development. For example, Point Reyes, not far from Drakes Bay, offers complete solitude, though it is only an hour's drive from the Golden Gate Bridge, while the university city of Berkeley, California's intellectual laboratory, offers lively streets, cafes and butiques.

Marin County and its symbol-city Sausalito lie on the north side of the Golden Gate Bridge. Marin County is many things: a nature reserve, an exclusive area for the rich who prefer a house in the countryside to the stress of city life, and a huge recreational area where many paths overlooking the ocean can be explored on bike or on foot.

However, there is more to Marin County than just Sausalito, for it also boasts small, wealthy towns like Mill Valley, Ross and the exclusive Belvedere Lagoon, not far from the San Francisco Yacht Club. Nonetheless, it is Sausalito and Belvedere (an artificial lagoon) that are best known for their classic, health-centered and alternative Californian way of life and as a place where many residents choose to live on houseboats. Today high property prices make the area affordable mainly to rich middle-class whites with their organic food, New Age practices, and luxury automobiles. Farther north, following Highway One toward Mount Tamalpais Park, famous for its lookout points and gigantic sequoia trees, the visitor arrives at Bolinas, a small town that has always tried to remain anonymous, in perfect symbiosis with the peace of Marin County. Just past Bolinas is Point Reyes, a long peninsula that Sir Francis Drake passed to enter the bay bearing his name. Here the coast is unspoiled, with scattered lighthouses, marine and terrestrial wildlife and paths and beaches where hikers and visitors are few.

Napa and Sonoma are two valleys roughly 50 miles northeast of San Francisco. Since the mid-19th century their fortunes have been linked to the international success of California's red and white wines. Surrounded by the mountains of the coastal chain, the landscape of the Napa and Sonoma valleys is characterized by huge expanses of vineyards and (at winter's end) the yellow flowers of the mustard plant. Hundreds of acres of vineyards have allowed 250 wineries to flourish, with the warm California sunshine ensuring large grape harvests. Though both exist on wine production, the two valleys have different styles. Napa draws international tourists, while Sonoma is more relaxed and its wine-making follows European traditions.

Berkeley lies on the other side of the Bay Bridge in the direction of the East Bay. The cultural and social hub of the area is the huge University of California campus with around 500 buildings and some 30,000 students. UC Berkeley is one of the world's most famous universities; in the 1960s the student leadership grabbed the headlines in demonstrating against American involvement in the Vietnam War. The symbols of this institution, which was founded in 1873, are the bell-tower and Sather Gate. Apart from its educational mission, the university is also an important research center in the spheres of both technology and political theory and social sciences. The Palo Alto area, south of San Francisco, is home to Stanford, the

122 and 123 from left to right Marshlands in the East Bay Area. Stanford University's rugby and athletics field. Oakland, with Lake Merritt on the downtown side. A tower of the Bay Bridge.

125 Close-up of the Bay Bridge. This double-decker bridge was completed in 1936, a year before the Golden Gate, and drastically reduced the number of boats plying the waters of the bay.

region's second great university. It was founded in 1891 and is one of the most prestigious institutions in the United States, with faculties ranging from medicine to scientific specializations focusing on research. Like Berkeley, Stanford has a huge campus, which features many Neoclassic-style buildings, a church and a large sports complex.

San Francisco's other metropolitan hub is Oakland, whose importance grew with the arrival of the transcontinental railway in 1869. Construction of the Bay Bridge at the end of the 1930s stimulated further growth, as did arms production during World War II. Like Berkeley, Oakland experienced political tensions that, at the end of the 1960s, increased sharply with the Afro-American Black Panther movement's struggle for racial rights.

This period also saw the opening of the Oakland Museum of California (1969) designed by Kevin Roche. Dedicated to art, nature and the history of California, the museum has three stories, with a roof garden for visitors above the lower one.

Features of Oakland are its "miniature" skyline, hardware and software industries and, above all, its gigantic goods depot that takes in and sends out container cargo from and to all ports in the Far East.

What makes Oakland famous throughout California, however, is its lively music scene, with clubs, concerts, music schools and recording stu-

dios. Jazz and blues are the most popular forms and one of the best-known venues is Yoshi's, a Japanese restaurant that has become a must-go for music-lovers in the Bay Area.

Leaving behind the Bay Area and heading toward Los Angeles along the spectacular Highway One that follows the Californian coastline, the visitor encounters Monterey and Carmel-by-the-Sea. Both these seaside towns are dedicated to tourism and pleasure boating. Monterey and its peninsula are also famous for their large aquarium, golf courses and protected natural habitat. Farther south is one of America's most beautiful areas: the 90-mile stretch of rocky coasts and promontories of the Big Sur ("the Big South"). The Big Sur is still largely untamed and can be visited from Highway One and, better still, its parks and their paths offer striking landscapes. The region is the retreat of intellectuals, millionaires and artists (first and foremost Henry Miller), who started arriving here after World War II, and has been conserved with farsightedness by the local authorities. Following the crowded summer season, the Big Sur returns to its solitary and highly evocative state, constantly enveloped in fog and scoured by the strong winds blowing in from the Pacific, ceaselessly rolling up against the rocky, wooded coast.

126 Tortuous Highway One runs along the 90-mile stretch of the Big Sur, a largely untamed coastal stretch between San Francisco Bay and the Greater Los Angeles Area.

127 The Big Sur ("the Big South") overlooks the Pacific Ocean. Part of the Big Sur is a protected nature reserve as the area boasts an extraordinarily rich flora and fauna.

128-129 Point Reyes, on the tip of the National Seashore Park of the same name, in Marin County, is one of the most scenic areas north of San Francisco. It is situated an hour's drive from the city along the spectacular Shoreline Highway.

130-131 and 132-133 The extensive Lake Merritt saltwater lagoon contributes to the high quality of life enjoyed by Oakland's inhabitants; its shores are lined with numerous parks and play areas.

131 top Oakland Stadium hosts the games of the local baseball team – the Oakland Raiders – and soccer matches.

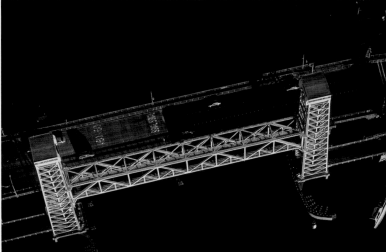

134-135 The Alameda County administrative offices, opposite Oakland, have the severe, linear design typical of government buildings. Beyond the complex, the outer lane of the freeway runs along a stretch of Lake Merritt's shore.

135 Nothing of the dizzy grandeur of San Francisco's bridges are found in the span that connects the mainland to Fruitvale Avenue in Alameda County, situated on a long island just south of Oakland.

136 top The University of California's branch in Berkeley, founded in 1868, soon became one of the most prestigious academic institutes in California and the entire United States.

136 bottom The Berkeley campus, which ring a 3-square-mile are, is dominated by the white Campanile.

136-137 Berkeley's Memorial Stadium, whose main entrance is shown here, hosts professional games and numerous college matches. It was opened in 1923 and has a capacity of 80,000 spectators.

137 top The Berkeley campus. Behind the stadium, the huge campus houses hundreds of academic and residential buildings.

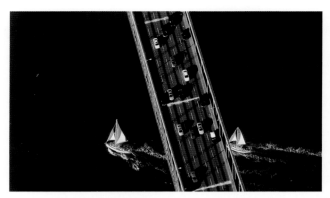

138 top Small craft sailing beneath a span of the Bay Bridge, running 197 feet bove the waterline.

138-139 The Bay Bridge, completed in 1936 (a year before the Golden Gate) was a great feat of engineering that enabled San Francisco to connect with towns inland across the bay.

139 right On average, 250,000 vehicles cross the Bay Bridge daily. This is an enormous number, but then all figures relating to this manmade wonder are breathtaking. For example, in 1933, during construction, the bridge required 6% of the US' total steel production for that year.

140 top Palm Drive, a mile-long palm-lined avenue connects Stanford University to Palo Alto.

140 bottom The Hoover Tower is
visible all over the Stanford campus. It was built in 1941 to celebrate the university's 50th anniversary. The 285-foot building houses a carillon of bells.

140-141 The Oval, at the end of Palm Drive, leads to Stanford's Main Quad, and Memorial Church (center of photograph). The church, which is the heart of the university, was consecrated in 1900, damaged by the 1906 earthquake, and
subsequently rebuilt around a steel framework.

141 top The enormous Stanford University campus in Palo Alto was founded in 1891 and consists of acre upon acre of greenery, athletic facilities, and dozens of buildings.

142, 143 top and 144-145 The Silicon Valley landscape is a mix of residential areas and high-technology businesses.

143 bottom San Francisco

International, founded in 1927, is still the city's airport.

146-147 The canals of Foster City, on Whaler's Island, are lined with attractive, expensive housing.

148

*148 and 148-149
In the East Bay,
the surprising
convergence of
lagoons, salt
marshes, and
mudflats seems to
trace abstract
patterns. The
colored effects are
created as the salt
marshes mingle
with the mud*

*sediments and
moving water of the
tidal channels.*

*150-151 Tightly-
packed residential
plots and marshes
alternate in the
mudflat area, creating
a unique landscape in
perfect equilibrium
between the water and
the land.*

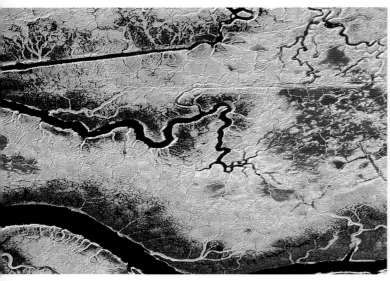

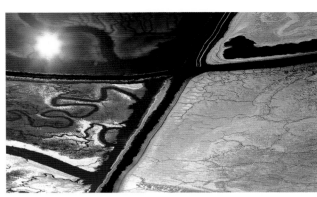

152 top Highway One climbs toward Mount Tamalpais Park, famous for its lookout points and gigantic sequoia trees.

152 bottom In the 1960s Sausalito's famous houseboats were the meeting place for the hippy community; they are now highly sought after by middle-class whites.

152-153 A long beach lines the coastal stretch accommodating the towns of Sausalito and Marin City. Both these upper-class residential areas face onto Richardson Bay, which in turn opens onto the larger San Francisco Bay a few miles north of the city.

154 top A bird's-eye view of dozens of seemingly tiny sailing boats crowding a stretch of Monterey Bay, south of San Francisco. Monterey is the capital of the county of the same name, which boasts the spectacular cliffs of the Big Sur, Pebble Beach and Carmel.

154-155 and 155 As shown by these two views of Monterey Marina, pleasure boating in the bay is one of the favorite pastimes of local residents, who benefit from the region's constantly mild climate.

156 top This wide southward view takes in several miles of the Big Sur coast, edged with cliffs.

156-157 Highway One runs along the rugged coast of the Big Sur, which is some spots falls sheer to the ocean. The inhabited areas that can be seen on the cliffs are the homes of wealthy owners who have chosen to live in this natural paradise.

157 right The road that runs alongside the Big Sur offers dizzy views over the ocean breakers.

158-159 The Big Creek arch bridge enables Highway One to proceed southward, toward Los Angeles. The Big Sur coast is one of America's most evocative landscapes; it is still largely untamed and much of it is a protected nature reserve.

160 The unmistakable silhouette of the symbolic Transamerica Pyramid dominates *the San Francisco skyline. The 853-foot building, completed in 1972, has 3,678 windows.*

The photographer would like to thank the pilot Michael C. Flaherty for his support.

PHOTO CREDITS

All the pictures inside the book are by Antonio Attini/Archivio White Star except for the following:
Alamy Images: page 8
World Sat: page 16
World Sat: page 17 top and bottom
Heeb/laif/Contrasto: pages 18-19
Alamy Images: pages 20-21
Richard Gross/Corbis/Contrasto: page 53 bottom
Robert Holmes/Corbis/Contrasto: pages 56-57
Jim Wark: pages 92-93